HERTFORDSHIRE
Volume 1 – South and West

A Portrait in Old Picture Postcards

by

Margaret and Roy Sturgess

S. B. Publications
1990

Dedicated to our daughter, Helen;
to remind her of the county in which she was born.

First published in 1990 by S. B. Publications
5 Queen Margaret's Road, Loggerheads, Nr. Market Drayton, Shropshire, TF9 4EP.

ISBN 1 870708 30 X

Typeset and printed by Geo. R. Reeve Ltd., Wymondham, Norfolk NR18 0BD.

CONTENTS

CONTENTS CONTINUED

S.B. Publications

INTRODUCTION

Nothing has been static or finite in the production of this volume. The whole project has grown from the original idea of taking a nostalgic look at the county. This idea was to expand a collection of postcards of one town into a collection depicting every village and town in Hertfordshire – although we knew that cards of this county are not as easy to find as those of other counties. We then planned to visit each location to note any changes that had taken place over the years. This, we thought, was the easy bit!

Months passed while notes were written "on the hoof" – hard to write at the time and harder to read later! Also, the acquisition of "new" postcards required revisits. Research went on continually, using standard works of reference and by correspondence. Our greatest asset turned out to be local folk in every place who were marvellous with directions, items of lore, legend, social history, names and anecdotes that filled our notebooks and minds.

Words become obsolete or fall into disuse; elements in the landscape follow the same pattern. Everywhere around us there are physical features – either complete or just fragments – that are no longer in use and are often ignored. These are captured on postcards – together with people who were born and raised under different circumstances and with different social habits. Their faces stare at us, captured in a moment of time. Postcards prompt our memories of earlier times. The images remain whilst the landscape changes.

The text includes details of the postcard, such as basic facts, dates and publishers, together with the historical background and changes and development at each location. Obtaining information about a whole county is not as easy as researching the facts about one's own town. County information tends to be split between various museums and libraries and not every area has access to newsprint. Finally, cards of some small villages and hamlets are rare and, when found, are often faded beyond reproduction. So far, we have managed to collect postcards of two-thirds of the places in Hertfordshire. We are grateful to those local photographers who recorded so much of the county at the beginning of this century, especially William Coles and the firm of Downer, both of Watford, whose cards have provided many illustrations for this volume.

INTRODUCTION (Contd.)

Please forgive us our mistakes! If any reader wants to correct or add to information or send cards of villages not illustrated, your contribution will be acknowledged gratefully. In this way, knowledge of the county will be expanded, and information will be passed on to various archivists. When we started this project, we simply enjoyed the cards; now we have extended that enjoyment to include everything about Hertfordshire. It has been fun to write and we hope that you derive as much pleasure from reading it.

Margaret and Roy Sturgess,
January 1990.

The sequence of postcards has been selected to follow a tour of the county. In this first volume we have started at the north-western corner and Tring, then along the A41 to King's Langley, visiting the villages on either side. Next is the south-western area and the larger towns of Rickmansworth, Bushey and Watford. From here we cross to Watling Street and go south to Elstree and Boreham Wood before taking the B5378 to our final destination, St. Albans. Volume 2 will begin from this point.

By the same authors:

Hertfordshire: Volume 2 – Central and South-East
Hertfordshire: Volume 3 – North and East

ALMOND BLOSSOM AT LONG MARSTON. HERTFORDSHIRE   The Times COPYRIGHT

ALMOND BLOSSOM AT LONG MARSTON, c. 1938

This rural scene, with horses in the road, is still typical of this corner of the county where a little piece of Hertfordshire juts into Buckinghamshire. The cottages on the left have gone, revealing another old dwelling behind and leaving room for a newer house to be built at right angles to the road. The postcard was a "freebee" to readers of The Times and is one of a series entitled "Spring Blossom"; it captures the fresh smell of springtime in an England soon to be engaged in war.

(Published by Photochrom Co. Ltd., London & Tunbridge Wells)

Wilstone Herts.

The Season's Greetings.

WILSTONE, c. 1905

A local lady suggested that this view may be of Church End Lane – a tight turning with various "Do Not . . ." and other similar notices. Unfortunately, this view could not be matched with today's scenery, probably because these wooden buildings would have been removed long ago. There is another cottage behind the trees in the distance. In Victorian times, barely 400 people lived at Wilstone and it fails to rate an entry in any reference book. The postcard was overprinted with a seasonal greeting but has lain unused for 80 years and now just baffles researchers!

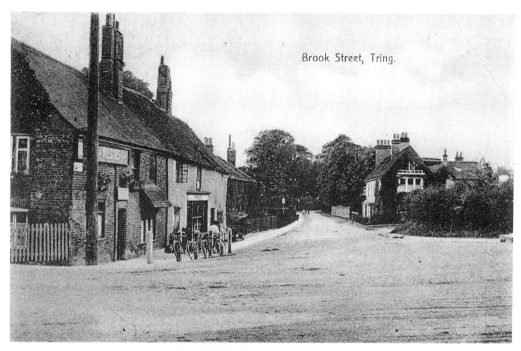

Brook Street, Tring.

BROOK STREET, TRING, c. 1910

When this postcard was sent in 1912, the writer described the town as "a pretty place . . . . picked a lot of blackberries on our way". The view has changed greatly for it is beached at the busy junction of the B488. The building on the right has been replaced by a filling station and modern flats. The buildings on the left have suffered a more drastic change – the Robin Hood is now obscured to the first floor by a pedestrian moat which leads to the few small shops beyond. The tree-lined road has now succumbed to modern development.

(Published by De Fraine & Co., Tring)

HIGH STREET, TRING, May, 1910

The flags are out and the crowds are gathered for the Proclamation of King George V. There was obviously much discussion about the new King and the lady in the centre has a look of excitement on her face. This postcard was sold by C. A. Howlett – only a few hundred were produced and not many have survived. On the left, on the corner of Frogmore Street, is F. & J. Smith's tobacconist's shop, where postcards can be clearly seen in the window as well as advertisements for various brands of tobacco; the shop is now a florist's. On the corner of Akenham Street is Jeffery's chemist's shop with a wall advertisement for Thorley's cattle food; this shop is still a chemist's shop today, but the name is changed to A. Smith.

Note the sign for the George Hotel in the left foreground – the hotel is not visible here and is now a boutique.

High Street, Tring.

S. G. Payne & Son, Aylesbury.

HIGH STREET, TRING, c. 1895

A photograph taken in the mid-1890s was used for this postcard which was not issued until after 1902. On the right-hand side, where a canvas booth and people can be seen on the pavement, is the newspaper office which was replaced by a mock-timbered building in c. 1897, so this picture must be earlier than that. On the left, Fulk's shop has a sale and has hats, shirts, bales of cloth and other white goods placed outside to tempt the passer-by, whilst next door, The Plough Hotel offers billiards. The Hotel is now a garden supplies shop and John Bly has an antiques shop in the same row.

(Published by S. G. Payne & Sons, Aylesbury)

5

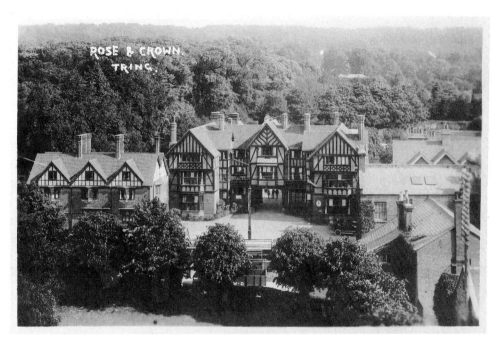

THE ROSE AND CROWN, TRING, c. 1905

From a vantage point at the top of the church opposite, this view must have been taken just after alterations were made to the inn. The building was given the pseudo half-timbered look that was so popular in the late Victorian and Edwardian periods. It was carried out for the Rothschild family of Tring Park, which can be seen behind the inn. Today, the arch at the front has been filled in, creating new reception facilities, and the building on the right has been altered; otherwise it is unchanged.

TRING PARK, c. 1910

This seventeenth-century house was designed by Sir Christopher Wren for Henry Guy and was bought by the Rothschild family in 1873. The left-hand wing and a top storey were added during the 1890s. The old walls were encased in red brick with pediments in 1915. The house is in the lovely setting of a 300-acre park and the view shows a herd of ostrich in the foreground. The wealthy Rothschild family were well-known for their philanthropy and interest in art and zoology. They did much for the town; the second Lord Rothschild set up the Zoological Museum which was bequeathed to the British Museum in 1938; the family founded an Arts Educational Trust; and also had many cottages built for their estate workers.

TRING CUTTING IN THE COURSE OF CONSTRUCTION, 1837

Tring is two miles from its railway which opened in 1837. The postcard, taken from a Bourne lithograph, shows the navvies at work and explains why it took two years to build up enough muscle to cope with the extreme physical task of moving mountains by hand. The way these men lived and worked – as a race apart from local people – is well documented. When the British railway network was complete, these men worked all over the world – *they were the best*. The card is from a set of six "Railway Cuttings" issued in January 1905, costing 6d. for the set. This one was sold in Wigan in 1906. Railway cards were popular and are still eagerly sought after.

(Published by the London & North Western Railway)

ALDBURY, TRING, HERTS.

Photo Copyright, J. T. NEWMAN, BERKHAMPSTED.

ALDBURY, c. 1905

About a mile from Tring station is the charming village of Aldbury. The scene has hardly changed over the years. Many delightful cottages cluster around the village green, seen here. There are stocks and a pond, where there was no doubt a ducking-stool; on this view there is a sign which warns "The pond at this end is DANGEROUS". There is a baker's cart outside the bakehouse, which has a tall chimney at the rear and where people could take their Sunday joint which could be roasted for a small fee. Just visible on Moneybury Hill, on the right, is the 1832 monument to the 3rd. Duke of Bridgewater, the famous canal pioneer. The manor house is on the left.

(Published by J. T. Newman, Berkhamsted)

STOCKS AND OLD HOUSES, ALDBURY, c. 1920

This lovely old building is the seventeenth-century manor house which overlooks the village pond and stocks. It is a fine timbered building with lattice windows. Most surprising is the fact that it does not rate an entry in Pevsner's guide. There are some other fine buildings in the village including the tiny seventeenth-century almshouses.

(Published by C. Dickens, Aldbury)

BRASSES OF SIR R. VERNEY & HIS WIFE, ST. JOHN THE BAPTIST CHURCH, ALDBURY, c. 1920

Postcards of brasses are rare and this is a particularly good one because the detail and elaborate patterns on the tabard and dress are so clear. Originally at Ashridge, the brasses came to this church in 1547. Sir Ralph's father, Sir John Verney was a Yorkist who married a staunch Lancastrian's daughter, so the Houses of York and Lancaster have come together in the same tomb. Sir Ralph and his wife had nine sons and three daughters, all of whom, like their parents, have magnificent brasses on the family tomb.

(Published by W. A. Call, Monmouth)

1547. Sir R. Verney and wife,
Aldbury, Herts.

11

ALDBURY, HERTFORDSHIRE.

ALDBURY FROM THE SOUTH-EAST, c. 1906

In 1949, the Penguin Guide stated ". . . . to see this village is to remember it". There are many postcard views of the village and this is one from the same set as that on page 9. The pictures were taken by J.T. Newman of Berkhamsted. This view shows the perfect setting of the community and was probably taken from half-way up Tom's Hill. There is a farmhouse in the foreground and the gig could well have belonged to Mr. Newman. On the horizon is the tumulus to the north-west of the village.

(Published by J. T. Newman, Berkhamsted)

ASHRIDGE PARK FROM THE AIR, LITTLE GADDESDON, c. 1938

This fine house is built on the site of a Norman monastery and was subsequently used as a home by the children of Henry VIII. By 1800, the house had fallen into decay and its owner, the 7th Earl of Bridgewater, commissioned James Wyatt to restore and rebuild the house in 1808. It is the largest of the romantic Gothic palaces near London and this aerial view clearly shows its symmetry. The house is now used as a business college. Capability Brown landscaped the garden in 1760, and his work emerges with Repton's added features, such as the sun rose garden, some fifty years later.

(Published by Aerofilms, Ltd., Hendon)

NORTHCHURCH VILLAGE, c. 1908

It should have been easy to locate this view which shows the George and Dragon Motor Garage on the left-hand side of the road. Unfortunately, the village has become merged into Berkhamsted and this road is now a busy street where one loiters at one's peril – not like the people in this view who were able to wander down the road without fear of being knocked down. However, the writer of this postcard does say that ". . . . mama will not cycle all that way alone" – referring to a journey from Berkhamsted to Aylesbury – so was obviously worried about the dangers.

(Published by E. Needham & Co.)

NORTHCHURCH CHURCH, c. 1908

The picture was taken by the same photographer as the last view, but was issued by a different publisher. Parts of the Church date from Saxon times but most of it is of more recent origin. The walls are of flint and the fifteenth-century tower is of Totternhoe stone. There are some good Victorian stained glass windows. A brass tablet commemorates a Hanoverian boy known as Peter the Wild Boy. An imbecile, he was brought to England by George I and, at first, was an object of interest to the nobility. Efforts to educate him failed and he spent the last years of his life with a collar, bearing his address in Berkhamsted, around his neck; he died in 1785 aged 72.

(Published by Loosley's Series, Berkhamsted)

The Castle & Palace of Berkhampstead in the time of King Edward IV.

BERKHAMSTED CASTLE

This sketch was probably drawn by a local historian, C. H. Ashdown, and shows Berkhamstead Castle in about 1471; the year Edward IV had regained the throne from Henry VI during the turbulent Wars of the Roses. The castle was unique in that it had three moats. The mounds jutting out into the outer moat were bastions and used to position mangonels – mediæval engines for throwing stones. Today, little remains of the building but visitors can see remnants of the walls, foundations, mound and earthworks. There is a new house where the granaries stood and railway lines across the entrance.
(The castle granaries were situated to the left of the inner gate-house)

HIGH STREET LOOKING NORTH, BERKHAMSTED, c. 1918

This is one of many good postcard views of the town. On the left is Chesham Road with the old seventeenth-century inn, The Swan, with the flagpole, on the corner. On the side wall there are several posters and advertisements. Further along the street is the King's Arms with three bay windows on the first floor. On the right-hand side, the Town Hall is in the distance and the row of houses in the foreground have been replaced by a new supermarket which manages to preserve the old roof line but on a grander scale. There are a number of horse-drawn vehicles to be seen but no motor traffic.

(Published by T.W.B. Series)

Photo Copyright.]   **REVIVAL OF BERKHAMPSTED MARKET.**   [J. T. Newman.
Messrs. W. Brown & Co.'s Sale in the High Street, to be continued every Tuesday.
The market dates from the year 1156, when a charter was granted by Henry II.

REVIVAL OF THE MARKET, HIGH STREET, BERKHAMSTED, c. 1908

The full caption reads "Messrs. W. Brown & Co.'s Sale in the High Streeet, to be continued every Tuesday. The market dates from the year 1156, when a charter was granted by Henry II." Although the caption refers to Tuesday markets, the ancient one was held on a Thursday. In fact, the picture does not show a market at all; Messrs. Brown are holding an auction in front of the Town Hall; auctions must have been held here since the town was known as Durobivae. Note the number of "coke" hats (bowlers) and the magnificent "beaver" (beard) on the man behind the lamp standard. The latter has lost its glass lantern – something for the copper to investigate, perhaps!

(Published by J. T. Newman, Berkhamsted)

18

HIGH STREET AND TOWN HALL, BERKHAMSTED, c. 1924

Looking in the opposite direction, this photograph is full of fine detail. On the left is W. Good's drapery and millinery with several bales of cloth on display outside and, on the pavement there is a trestle-table laden with plants and flowers. The shop has a delightful sign above the window which must have been painted by a master signwriter. Next is the Town Hall and just beyond that is the White Hart Commercial Hotel. On the edge of the pavement outside the Hotel there is a fancy lamp standard and horse trough. Most of the buildings shown here have been replaced by larger stores and the Town Hall is now the Town Hall Shopping Arcade.

TRAVELLING ENTERTAINERS, HIGH STREET, BERKHAMSTED, 1840

This is a good example of the use of an early photograph for a postcard. The caption states that the photograph dates from 1840 but it has been suggested that a more likely date would be 1860, and the postcard was not issued until at least 1902. The message on the back reads "Sarah Ann says very likely you would remember this – I bought it purposely for you". The picture shows a crowd of people – of all ages – engrossed in the antics of Punch and Judy. The booth has been set up in the roadway and would have been a delightful diversion for the townsfolk. At the time the population was just 5,000.

LOWER KINGS ROAD, BERKHAMSTED, c. 1953

Here is a view that many people will remember. The cars are the focal point – typical family runabouts of the period that will prompt the phrase: "we had one of those!" When the picture was taken the row of shops was fairly new but, now, the awnings have gone and many of the shops are to let. The one on the corner, with the clock, is presently occupied by Bookstack. On the opposite corner, Pike's is still a greengrocer's but under a different name. The building in the right foreground has been demolished and replaced.

(Published by Valentine & Sons Ltd., Dundee)

WATERCRESS, ST. JOHN'S WELL LANE, BERKHAMSTED, c. 1904

These cultivators are growing green or summer watercress, which flourishes in river or canal water. Constant picking improved the plants and kept the flowers down, as allowing these to bloom lessened the flavour. Hertfordshire was only one of seven counties growing large quantities of watercress for sale to London. Now, Hertfordshire growers have lost out to Southampton in this market, although the plant is still found in small streams. Avoid it, as it can carry liver-fluke! The men in this picture are happy to take a break and pose for the cameraman – it must have been back-breaking work. A stack of packed boxes is ready for loading on to the carrier's cart.

(Published by J. T. Newman, Berkhamsted)

Railway Station, Berkhamsted.

THE RAILWAY STATION, BERKHAMSTED, c. 1908

The station was on the London & North Western Railway line to London, Euston and Broad Street. Today, there is not such an open aspect as in this view. A forecourt car park and a temporary building crowd the entrance. The brickwork, with its refined simple detail, is still impressive. Electrification is under way. Beyond the station-master's house there is some new property in a burgundy-coloured brick. The Grand Junction Canal is in the foreground. At the time of this view, a first-class return ticket to Broad Street cost 8/- (40p); a cheap half-day return was available on certain trains on Wednesdays and Saturdays for 2/6 (12½p). How times change!

(Published by Loosley & Sons, Berkhamsted)

HERTS IMPERIAL YEOMANRY CAMP AT BERKHAMSTED, MAY, 1906.

DOWNER, WATFORD.

HERTS. IMPERIAL YEOMANRY CAMP AT BERKHAMSTED, May 1906

When the Boer War started, a company of the 105-year-old Herts. Yeomanry Cavalry joined the Imperial Yeomanry. An article in Harmsworth Magazine at that time asks "Is the uniform doomed?", and talks of "commonplace khaki" but agreed that it was suitable in the field; however, a loss of "esprit de corps" was expected in peace time if the full dress uniform vanished. By 1906, as the postcard shows, "commonplace khaki" had won and the regiment's scarlet tunics and white metal helmets of 1896 were merely ceremonial.

(Published by Downer, Watford)

FINE ART PUBLISHING CO.

WATFORD.

INNS OF COURT O.T.C., BERKHAMSTED.

INNS OF COURT O.T.C., BERKHAMSTED, c. 1915

During World War 1, the Inns of Court Officers' Training Corps used the castle grounds as a gunnery school. This squad of 200 men cheerfully submit to their officer. The card has some pencil notes on the reverse, they appear to read "B or No 2 Coy Kenyon (Officer) Chetwynd Stapleton". On Berkhamsted Common there is an obelisk to the memory of two thousand officer cadets who gave their lives for their country during World War 1. Berkhamsted School lost 212 Old Boys during the war. A quotation from Berkhamsted's most famous son, the poet William Cowper (1731–1800), seems appropriate: "Where once we dwelt our name is heard no more".

(Published by Fine Art Publishing Co., Watford)

INNS OF COURT O.T.C. RUNNING TEAM, BERKHAMSTED, February 1917

Students of history would wager that every member of this team carries in his head the concept of "King and Country backed by God and the Commonwealth" – a cause worth dying for. This was the third year of World War 1 and was a serious time, so only one person here can raise a half-smile – or maybe it was the thought of the forthcoming run on what appears to be snow-covered ground! At least they all look determined and are clad in a motley array of shorts, shirts and plimsolls.

(Published by J. T. Newman, Berkhamsted)

BOURNE END LANE, BOURNE END, c. 1938

This is the view as seen from the end of the lane in 1938 – a quiet residential area. Today, the area on the left is occupied by the sizeable premises of J. W. Ward, Bourne End Mills, and there are cars everywhere. Quince Cottage, opposite, has new doors and windows but, otherwise, the row looks no different today.

(Published by The R.A.P. Co. Ltd., London)

WELL END, BOURNE END, c. 1927

Driving is tight in this small lane. In this view, the Post Office is beside the telegraph pole on the right-hand side and the church and the village pub are opposite. The cottages have changed but not greatly although new houses have been built in every available space.

THE SHANTY, BOURNE END, c. 1938

Just a mile from this spot one would be in Buckinghamshire. Situated off the busy A41, on the way to Boxmoor, the Shanty sprang to life on Saturday nights when it was the venue for the weekly "hop" – note the poster on the tree on the left, advertising a dance. The Café next door served teas and lunches and has a sign which reads "Teas & Hovis". The Shanty has been demolished and replaced by a filling station.

(Published by The R.A.P. Co. Ltd., London)

LONDON ROAD, BOXMOOR, c. 1910

Further along the A41, this view of the Swan Inn is a total contrast to the scene today. The Inn is still there, at the junction of London Road and Box Lane, on a cramped site with a packed car park and continuous traffic past the door. At the time of this picture the Inn was obviously a favourite with carters as a horse trough has been provided on the edge of the forecourt; the tree-lined road is so quiet it looks more like a path through a park. The cottage next door is now obscured by walls and trees – its presence almost beyond detection.

(Published by Valentine & Sons, Dundee)

FISHERY ROAD, BOXMOOR, c. 1905

The road now leads to a very busy roundabout which has altered this view beyond all recognition. In the 1920s, a house was built on the patch of garden on the extreme right of the picture; most of the trees have now gone. In the distance is the Common. An advertisement of 1910 announces the building of the Felden Estate at Boxmoor – "This Estate of over 40 acres, surrounded by Commons and adjoining Golf Links, is reserved for houses not costing less than £1,000, on sites of 1 acre and upwards. The price of land being only £350 per acre . . . . Main Drainage, Gas, Telephone, and constant Water Supply. Houses would be built for Tenants' requirements". It may seem inexpensive today, but at the time £1,000 was a considerable sum.

Something for You from **HEMEL HEMPSTEAD**

Within this postman's bag you'll find
An interesting gift consigned

973

"SOMETHING FOR YOU FROM HEMEL HEMPSTEAD", c. 1920

The postman's bag has a flap which opens to reveal a concertina of six small views of the town. The card is what is known as a stock card – one that was published for general use and overprinted with the name of the town in which it would be sold; the appropriate strip of pictures would then be affixed beneath the flap.

(Published by Valentines, Dundee)

HEH 16 THE TOWN ENTRANCE, HEMEL HEMPSTEAD A TUCK CARD

THE TOWN ENTRANCE, HEMEL HEMPSTEAD, c. 1950

This is the southern entrance to the town, at the approach to the roundabout where the A41, A414 and A4146 converge – the roundabout sign can be seen in front of the tree on the right. This entrance is flanked by green spaces and the River Gade which is clogged with a Hertfordshire staple – watercress. In 1982, new oak trees, gifted by various donors, were planted for National Tree Week; these look well for the future.

(Published by Raphael Tuck & Sons Ltd., London)

33

THE BROADWAY, HEMEL HEMPSTEAD, c. 1905

The picture was taken looking towards High Street. The black and white block of shops and houses, on the left, would have been a fairly recent construction – another example of the pseudo-Tudor style that was so popular at the turn of the century. The first shop appears to be a dress shop and, next door, a grocery with the shopkeeper in a white apron, standing in the doorway.

(Published by Valentine & Sons, Dundee)

HIGH STREET, HEMEL HEMPSTEAD, c. 1906

The street is viewed here from the junction with The Broadway, off to the left. From H. T. Clarke's bakery, on the left, and the imposing Bank building, on the right, the street meanders up the hill with a delightful mixture of old cottages, public houses and small shops on either side. This picture was obviously not taken on a school day as there are many children about. Several boys and girls are carrying baskets, others are just chatting – but all of them seem to be fascinated by the photographer.

(Published by Valentine & Sons, Dundee)

MARKET SQUARE AND TOWN HALL, HEMEL HEMPSTEAD, c. 1903

The neo-Jacobean Town Hall is constructed of red brick with stone dressings; it has some nineteenth-century additions. On the right is the market-place with the wall and entrance to the churchyard behind it. On the left-hand side is the Old Commercial Inn and Posting House. After World War 2, the town was developed as a New Town, with a modern town centre constructed in the 1950s and 1960s, adjoining the old town on its eastern edge.

(Published by Valentine & Sons, Dundee)

36

High Street, Hemel Hempstead.

Find Mummy.

HIGH STREET, HEMEL HEMPSTEAD, c. 1903

What a quiet street this was! There is hardly a soul in sight. In the right foreground is the old street pump, dated 1848, which has been ingeniously used to support a gas lamp. In the centre of the view there is a horse and cart, several workmen and building materials, and scaffolding has been erected against the facade of the Sun Inn, dated 1726. The side wall of the Town Hall can just be seen in the distance. Behind the right-hand rooftops is the 200ft-high leaded spire of St. Mary's Church which is a large Norman structure, although the spire was not built until the fourteenth century.

((Published by Bedford Series)

Gadebridge Lane, Hemel Hempstead

GADEBRIDGE LANE, HEMEL HEMPSTEAD, c. 1920

This is still a rural part of the town. The Lane cuts across the green at the top of the town's approach road from the north. When the picture was taken it was also the way to the army camp – the men on the little bridge over the Gade are in uniform and three mounted soldiers are approaching the camera. Today, this entrance has shoulder-high walls.

(Published by Valentine & Sons, Dundee)

THE FIRE AT GADDESDON PLACE, 1st 1905.
Downer. copyright.

THE FIRE AT GADDESDON PLACE, GREAT GADDESDON, 1st February, 1905

The House is just north of Hemel Hempstead. The household had smelt burning for days but little was done and, as a result, fire broke out in the house at 4 a.m. on February 1st. All efforts to save the house were in vain. Hemel Hempstead fire brigade laid 560 yards of hose and failed to quell the flames. A further 630 yards of hose reached another pond but the supply could not cope with a fire that was so fierce that it melted the lead on the roof. Paxton, the butler, and Jones, a footman, died in the cellar whilst attempting to save the wine. Very few of the house's contents were saved. The postcard uses an artist's impression to illustrate the disaster.

(Published by Downer, Watford)

THE VILLAGE, BEDMOND, c. 1908

The village is called Belmont in the 1870 gazetteer and is so small that it is not marked on some guides or maps, making this faded gem of a card a rarity. On the left-hand side, the little cottages have undergone some small improvements – there is a porch to No. 36 – but this has not changed the overall look of the row. The triangular chimney-breast, in the distance, identifies The Bell public house. On the right-hand side, all the buildings have gone, replaced by 1930s and 1940s villas and the village hall. The village was the birthplace of Nicholas Breakspear who became the only English pope, Adrian IV.

(Published by Coles, Watford)

THE VILLAGE, ABBOTS LANGLEY, c. 1917

On the left is the lychgate to St. Lawrence the Martyr's Church, a building of great architectural interest. Opposite is the King's Head public house selling Salter's Fine Ales and there are several small shops further along the street. These shops are still small shops today but the rest of the street has changed completely. The village is now embedded in a circular conglomeration of modern houses; the King's Head is a modern one-storey building, set back from the road, selling keg bitter instead of fine ales, and the house beyond is the Rose & Crown – without the white fence. The card bears a strange message – "Milly is singing under the More tree in the Gardens . . ." – it is hoped that the recipient understood this!

THE 'OVALTINE' FACTORY IN A COUNTRY GARDEN

AERIAL VIEW OF THE 'OVALTINE' DAIRY FARM

AERIAL VIEW OF THE 'OVALTINE' EGG FARM

THE OVALTINE FACTORY, KING'S LANGLEY, c. 1938

Drive past this 1930s model factory today and the circular dairy farm looks rather dilapidated. This comes as quite a shock to those who, as children, regularly listened to the radio programme with the much-loved tune – "We are the Ovaltineys . . .". Following the example of other enlightened employers, such as Cadbury's and Lever Bros., the Ovaltine Factory was built in the countryside to create a pleasant working environment. The facilities for the staff were obviously excellent – note the tennis court in the top picture. The Dairy Farm and Egg Farm were built to provide the necessary ingredients for their popular beverage.

THE MILL BRIDGE, KING'S LANGLEY, c. 1904

Because the bridge made it a tight turn for lorries, the road has been widened necessitating the removal of the flint-walled garden on the left. In recent years a modern factory has replaced the house behind the garden. On the right, the conservatory has been superseded by an extension to the house. The ford has been unused since the bridge was built. Today, the bank is completely overgrown and a large iron pipe runs parallel to the bridge, over the water. Urbanisation has struck a fatal blow at this once rural spot.

(Published by Wrench Series and W. Baldwin, King's Langley)

Kings Langley. Langley Hill.

LANGLEY HILL, KING'S LANGLEY, c. 1902

This is the view on the crest of the contours by Langley Lodge Farm, with these few houses dotted about. The old gentleman is standing on a patch of land that has now been landscaped. He has his back to the ruins of a thirteenth-century royal palace where Edmund de Langley was born in 1341 and became the first Duke of York. The village takes its name from the palace. Today, it is just a few crumbling remains but, when this picture was taken, it was still possible to find fragments of the tessellated floors.

(Published by Wrench Series and W. Baldwin, King's Langley)

Coombe Hill School, Kings Langley Priory, Herts.

COOMBE HILL SCHOOL, KING'S LANGLEY, c. 1910

What a lovely Edwardian social history card! Close by the royal palace there was a thirteenth-century Dominican friary that became the greatest house of its order in England. Bought in 1905–07 by a Miss Cross, it was opened as the Priory School and known as the "Green School" because the pupils wore green dresses. In the 1920s, after a change of management, Rudolph Steiner's theories were tested here; it was then called the "Red School" for the same reason as before. It is reputed to be a progressive school for children of free spirits.

(Published by P. A. Buchanan & Co., Croydon)

CHIPPERFIELD, c. 1905

This splendid common was almost 40 acres in area at the time of this picture. It is still a picturesque spot today and the common is larger as a further 113 acres were added in the 1930s, a gift of the Blackwell family. Sit with one's back to the church or the pub and enjoy the unspoiled view. Cottages and houses are neat and trim and, for the most part, unchanged. Horses canter past local residents having a lunchtime snack with their children. Crisps and a can of fizzy drink would have been a novelty to the two small children eyeing the cameraman from a distance!

(Published by H. W. Flatt, Boxmoor)

The Hounds, Chipperfield Common.

W.H.A. 2804.

THE HOUNDS, CHIPPERFIELD COMMON, c. 1910

Hunting had its detractors in 1910 – as now – but it is so tightly woven into the pattern of the English country life that we view this type of photograph as social history. Although hardly visible, the pack of hounds are behind the spectators, around the tree! Local schoolchildren have turned out to watch the horses, riders and hounds and see them on their way. Note the neat white pinafores worn by all the girls and the smart collars and caps of the boys. The common is a brisk walk away from the Grand Junction Canal and the narrow-boat people could have come here to watch the Hunt or, in summer, cricket being played on the pitch behind the oak tree – now blasted but growing again.

THE VILLAGE, BUCKS HILL, c. 1925

This photograph could have been taken anytime for this hamlet between Chipperfield and Bucks Hill Bottom is so small that time has stood still. The only clue to the date is the motor vehicle outside the inn. Victorian flint cottages and the pub sit on the edge of a five-mile square of peace and tranquility. Long may it be so.

CHIPPERFIELD. BOVINGTON ROAD.

Coles, Photographer, Watford.

BOVINGDON ROAD, c. 1905

William Coles of Watford captured this rural remnant of England on the road west from Chipperfield. He worked from 1890 to 1926, recording life around Watford on foot, by horse and by rail. Today, this road has a smattering of houses – but no ladies gathering sticks, wearing a bonnet and boots. It emphasises that rural England was never rich; it is recorded that the vicar of Chipperfield was managing on a living of £174 per annum in late Victorian times.

(Published by W. Coles, Watford)

BOVINGDON, c. 1905

The white cottage in the centre is The Bell; still open today. However, at the head of the High Street, significant changes have taken place and a timbered shop fills the green. In the left foreground, all the trees have gone together with the old well which can be seen behind the couple. Further along the grass verge, where all the young girls are gathered, is the "pixie hat" which now stands in the middle of the crossroads. It seems that all the young residents of the village have turned out for the photographer!

BOVINGDON, c. 1954

This postcard shows buildings that have already gone even though the photograph was only taken shortly after World War 2. The message mentions the Greenline bus to Boxmoor, on route 316. Postcard collectors are looking for cards of this era as it is realised that these views already show drastic changes in the landscape – sometimes more drastic than the changes that took place between the Edwardian period and World War 2. There were only a small number of firms publishing postcards in the 1950s and only a few enthusiasts collected them. The hobby became popular again in the early 1970s and is thriving today.

FLAUNDEN, c. 1908

Flaunden lies in the Chess valley and is renowned for its beauty. It has a Gilbert Scott church, a chapel, a ruined church and two good farmhouses. The inhabitants have lived their lives for a millenium without complaint – only venturing out of the locality to find a partner. Haystacks are becoming a thing of the past: straw now comes in rolls or black cylinders. Here, two men are taking a pride in their work whilst the horse waits patiently for the next load.

SARRATT GREEN, SARRATT, c. 1908

Sarratt has a long, quiet, undulating green which, in 1910, had more grass than road; however, it is still a very relaxed place today. The old cottage on the right is quaint, with an altered gable. The Wheatsheaf is seen on the left. Approximately 700 people lived in Sarratt a hundred years ago, with some of the inhabitants employed in fancy trimming and making paper. The message on the card, sent in August 1910, reads, " . . . We have all been to Abbots Langley Flower Show today, in the same brake as we went to Tring . . . N.G.H."

(Published by Coles, Watford)

THE WHEATSHEAF INN, SARRATT, SARRATT GREEN.

PROPRIETOR. H. GRIFFEN.

THE WHEATSHEAF INN, SARRATT, c. 1914

This lovely little inn faced the long village green. The landlord was Henry Griffen and maybe the couple standing at the doorway are Henry and his wife. The postcard has his name on the bottom right-hand corner so it was probably sold to his customers. On the wall, there is an enamel sign for the Daily Chronicle and another on the fence for Thorley's calf meal. Sadly, it is no longer an inn but the flint stone has preserved the facade and the empty frame for the inn sign remains. The cottages have either been extended or had a few minor alterations. The card was sent on 4th August, 1914 – the day that war was declared, and the day after pound notes replaced gold sovereigns.

THE CHURCH OF THE HOLY CROSS, SARRATT, c. 1910

The Church of the Holy Cross is situated a short distance from the village green. Any church over 900 years old is worth visiting and this church is certainly no exception. It had a totally different appearance before its extensive restoration in 1865 by Gilbert Scott who was responsible for many church restorations. At the time, the restorers discovered part of the earlier church had been constructed with Roman bricks. The many interesting features of the church include the unusual saddlebeam roof of the church tower, the mediæval carving on the tower arch, and the Norman font.

(Published by Coles, Watford)

Old Houses and Post Office, Chenies.

OLD HOUSES AND POST OFFICE, CHENIES, c. 1906

The village, which now lies in Buckinghamshire, is named after the Cheyne family and has a good manor and thirteenth-century church. It was often known as the model village of the Duke of Bedford. It is still a place worth a visit – an unspoilt village that looks the same today as on this postcard. As can be seen, the picturesque cottages are grouped around the green on which there are some fine elm trees. The sender of this card was staying at No. 43 and wrote . . . . "I have sent you a view of the house where we are lodging getting on alright" – a writer's cliché of the time.

(Published by Coles, Watford)

CHORLEYWOOD COMMON, CEDARS COTTAGE.

Coles, Photographer, Watford

CEDARS COTTAGE, CHORLEY WOOD COMMON, c. 1908

Extensive gorse commons surround the village of Chorley Wood. This area of common, by the Black Horse, is no longer grazed by sheep. Cedars Cottage has lost its ivy, cut down the trees, built a garage – and never hangs out washing in the front garden. Behind the trees there is a special school for the handicapped. There is also some new housing – like "The Stocks" – which has blended in well. It is still a place to stop, walk, make a sketch or simply enjoy the view.

(Published by Coles, Watford)

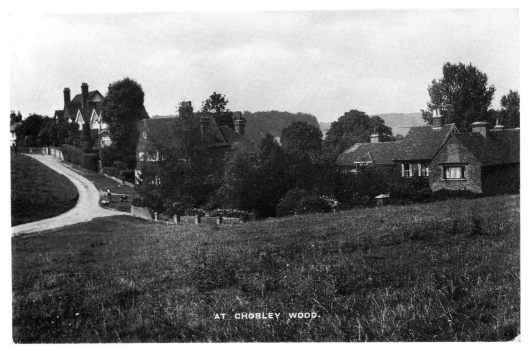

AT CHORLEY WOOD, c. 1920

The woods lie on the other side of this stretch of common, which serves the northern part of the town. These desirable residences were some of the first to creep into a green belt – making them targets for the pen of John Betjeman. Chorley, on the Buckinghamshire/Hertfordshire border, must have been particularly attractive to those able to pay the considerable sums needed to build this kind of property after World War 1 – sturdy houses that set a standard modern houses fail to match. A man is mowing the grass verge in front of the houses, everywhere is neat and tidy – nothing changes here.

Chorley Wood.

THE STATION, CHORLEY WOOD, c. 1912

Although this card is undated, it must be pre-1918 for it is stated on the reverse that a ½d. stamp is needed and the rates were increased in June 1918. In 1870, Chorley Wood's population of a thousand residents was served by Rickmansworth station so, when the railway came to Chorley, residential development soon followed. This scene looks quite bare and the houses new. According to a guide book of 1910: "This is a modern residential settlement, with many nice middle-class houses extending along one side of a steep hill and facing the wood; others being grouped round the railway station". Today, after driving round a curious dog-leg of a road, past the station, this open aspect is obscured by trees, fences and new buildings.

SOLESBRIDGE LANE, CHORLEY WOOD, c. 1904

This uncommon card shows a row of houses which are to the left-hand side of a busy junction leading to south Chorley Wood. Being a row, they have resisted change, but the picket fence has gone because the metalling has raised the level of the road.

CHORLEY WOOD

THE SWILLETT.

THE SWILLET, CHORLEY WOOD, c. 1914

It is most unlikely that this photograph is later than 1914, although the postcard is postmarked September, 1934. The Swillet is an area not a road. The Dove has a sign for Weller's Entire so the pub probably sold beer only – no spirits. The inclined seating on either side of the door must have become a slide to the over-the-eight drinkers! At the end of the road, the stores has all manner of goods on display, both inside and outside the shop. The Dove is now a private house and there has been much in-filling of housing; cars parked on either side of the road make progress difficult for drivers today.

Maple Cross, Rickmansworth.　　　　　　　　　Published by E. S. Brown, Rickmansworth.

MAPLE CROSS, RICKMANSWORTH, c. 1906

A few miles from Rickmansworth, off to the right at the Chalfont road junction, one will find four raggle-taggle yew trees, fronting a short row of modern shops – with housing everywhere else. Originally, these trees stood outside an eighteenth-century house that has been replaced. Yew clipped in this fashion dates from the Reformation; John Evelyn, the diarist, claims credit for its introduction. These marvellous topiary trees, "cut out with curious order" have many tiers – the tallest has fourteen tiers!

(Published by E. S. Brown, Rickmansworth)

THE VINE, MILL END, RICKMANSWORTH, c. 1909

This spot is a mile out of Rickmansworth. The Vine is on the left and opposite is Halsey's grocery shop and the premises of C. G. Horwood, a contractor who hired out steam-rollers – the ultimate in d.i.y! An abandoned plan to widen the road meant that the locals neglected to maintain the properties on the left. These have now fallen prey to a developer who has cleared a considerable area, including the demolition of the 'Vine', for the construction of retirement homes. On the left, notice the lovely patterned, etched glass – and example of good craftsmanship lost forever.

(Published by L. Stelling, Mill End)

UNITED PARADE, MILL END, RICKMANSWORTH, 7th July, 1907

The Chalfont Band are seen here at the Whip & Collar, Mill End. There is a full turnout for the occasion. The band arrived in the carts that have been fitted with long benches. Unfortunately, the words on the banner are not legible, but it would seem that this was to be a march of trade unionists or of members of a brotherhood or fellowship. In the foreground, P.C. 176 watches the men assemble whilst the other officer shouts instructions to the crowd. The pub now has a new sign and a mass of flowers during the summer months. The house beyond has been replaced by new houses. The railings in the right foreground have now been removed.

HIGH STREET, RICKMANSWORTH, c. 1907

A rare photographic postcard showing a wealth of detail. On the left is the Cart & Horses with fancy, etched windows and, next door, a butcher's shop with meat hanging over an open counter – the usual practice at the time. On the right-hand side there is a sign for Ford Motors and Cycles; the Queens Arms and a 1906 tourer – AR952 – very like the one the local newspaper used. Everyone has stopped for the photographer – a girl with a pram, a delivery boy, a young man in leggings carrying books and a parcels delivery man. Today, the Cart & Horses is a chemists. On the right, all the buildings before the twin gables have been replaced by Boots and other shops.

(Published by Warren Photo, Watford)

OLD COACHING YARD. SWAN HOTEL. RICKMANSWORTH

SWAN HOTEL YARD, RICKMANSWORTH, c. 1930

Rickmansworth's eastern entrance has lost much of its old housing. The Swan Hotel had a Jacobean staircase, panelling and fireplaces. Being an old coaching inn, its golden days faded with the coming of the railway in 1862. The Hotel was demolished in 1966.

(Published by T. J. Price, Rickmansworth)

6159   STATION ROAD, RICKMANSWORTH.

STATION ROAD, RICKMANSWORTH, c. 1906

On the right-hand side, Ibbotson's has been modernised and, beyond, there are four modern shop units and then Penn Place – all blinds and blue panels. This in turn is doomed, with local residents objecting to plans for office development. On the left, modern shop-fronts have been incorporated under unchanged upper floors. Closer inspection shows the following detail – "Boots soled and heeled, Gents 2/6d, Ladies 1/6d;" a man with an umbrella and Gladstone bag; another man has a Jack Russell; drainpipes on the cart; two dyers and cleaners; one florist; and seven young girls, their faces and dress showing the class differences of the time.

(Published by W. H. Smith, Kingsway Series, London)

BATCHWORTH LOCKS, RICKMANSWORTH, c. 1909

Two boats are being negotiated through the locks on the marvellous system that was the Grand Junction Canal. These boatmen were a special breed who saw both the industrial scene and the countryside: the dirt and the tranquility. The lock-keepers were also a special breed; Arthur Mee records four generations of one family at this lock – the great-grandfather for 62 years; the grandfather for 58; the father for 41 and the son for 31 – nearly 200 years service between them. This is another railway company card, taken from a set of 6, costing 2d. per set, showing views on the line from Northwood to Chorley Wood, with the name of the nearest station printed on the card.

(Published by the Metropolitan Railway Company)

THE VILLAGE, CROXLEY GREEN, c. 1904

Benjamin H. Ward kept the shop offering the best of everything, ran the post office – with ten collections a day – and probably employed the coy delivery boy. Despite such a heavy workload, he still found time to publish his own postcards of the area! At the junction are Berean Cottages with All Saints Church behind. Today, traffic is anything but leisurely at this roundabout by Rickmansworth School. A steel railing outside the shop confirms this; it is now occupied by Allsorts, hobbies and bric-a-brac dealer. Modern blinds hang at Q. D. Goldsmith's shop, replacing the old-style wider blinds with their metal struts, which small boys would swing at their peril!

(Published by B. H. Ward, Croxley Green)

BEREAN COTTAGES, CROXLEY GREEN, c. 1903

People who use the Hall on this site in front of All Saints Church may be interested in one of the original residents of the almshouses. Built in 1837, they were known as "Penny Row" because the rent for the little old lady in this view was one penny a week – 4/4d (22p) per year! This rose to 1/- (5p) a week, for the ex-servicemen who rented the cottages after World War 1. Naturally, the name was changed to Heroes Terrace. In 1932, the almshouses closed and a new Hall was built on the site; the land having been given up by the charity run by C. Morland Agnew.

HIGH STREET, BUSHEY, c. 1920

HIGH STREET, BUSHEY, c. 1920

A varied selection of transport is seen here: an open-topped bus on route 142; a motor-cycle combination and a horse-drawn delivery van. It is this sort of detail that makes postcards expensive today. On the right-hand side are: Finches' confectionery shop, the Robin Hood public house, selling Benskins Ales; and further along, the Red Lion. The uncluttered look of the street has, like so many others, been destroyed by traffic lights, "quaint" weather-boarding, national logos and the like. The Robin Hood pub is now a pharmacy and the Red Lion has a black and white mock-Tudor design.

THE OLD FORGE, BUSHEY, c. 1915

The old forge was in the centre of town, possibly by St. James' Church – a church building is just visible on the extreme right of the picture. The forge disappeared long ago, depriving the local children of hours of innocent pleasure watching a latter-day Vulcan at work. The building was a reminder of the small village that Bushey once was. Not only was it considered to have an environment of considerable natural beauty but, in 1908, its population of 6,500 had the lowest death-rate in England!

(Published by S. Giles, Bushey)

ROYAL MASONIC SCHOOL BUSHEY

A.R.B

THE ROYAL MASONIC SCHOOL, BUSHEY, c. 1905

The Royal Masonic School illustrated by a watercolour, painted by an artist with the initials A.R.B. Built in 1902, the school is a mixture of styles with Tudor, Gothic and even a touch of Art Nouveau – found in the pavilion roof. It gives an education to children of the Masonic Order. Science and art and craft blocks were added in 1967 and a music school in 1974. Bushey has always attracted artists who painted up on Bushey Heath – until it became built upon. J. M. W. Turner's connection with Thomas Hearne, the eighteenth century water-colourist, and Hubert Herkomer's famous School of Art reinforce the town's artistic tradition.

OMNIBUS LH 8479, WATFORD, c. 1912

"What is this that roareth thus? Can it be a Motor Bus? Yes, the smell and hideous hum, Indicat Motorem Bum" – A. D. Godley's jingle could have been written for this vehicle on route 142: Kilburn High Road via Bushey to Watford High Street (see page 70). The bus is a solid-tyred, "B" type, 34-seater belonging to the London General Omnibus Company who concentrated on the London routes. The "B" type ran at least until 1926, confirmed by photographs of the General Strike. It left the driver exposed to the weather and had the main body of the bus over the rear wheels. The new "K" type, a 46-seater, shielded the driver and had the main body over all four wheels.

AN APRIL SNOWSTORM, CASSIOBURY PARK GATES, WATFORD, 24th April, 1908

In 1545, Sir Richard Morrison bought Cashio, a hamlet of Watford parish, and built Cassiobury, home of the Earls of Essex until 1922. It was one of the county's major architectural losses of this century. The Lodge gates, built in 1802, survived until 1970. This snow scene was the result of a blizzard which affected most of Britain on 24th and 25th April, 1908. Several feet of snow fell and many places were cut off. Local photographers quickly produced postcards which were on sale within hours. This one was sent on 29th April, with no mention of the weather – unusual for an Englishman! Unsold cards had a seasonal greeting added and were used as Christmas cards.

(Published by Watford Engraving Co.)

Watford Market Place after the Great Storm, July 27th, 1906. *Downer*

THE GREAT STORM, WATFORD, 1906

At one o'clock on Friday, 27th July, 1906, a heavy thunderstorm caused flash floods in the Watford area. The postcard shows the Market Place after the storm, with the flood water at a depth of 6 inches. Market Street was flooded to 3 inches and, nearby, the electricity sub-station had water to a depth of 8 feet 6 inches. Among the many incidents which were reported at the time were: the electric light works were closed for four hours; Mr. P. Buck lost goods stored in his cellars in the High Street; and lightning killed three sheep at Cassiobury Park. When the lightning stuck the nearby manor house, all the electric bells were started and had to be disconnected.

(Published by Downer, Watford)

MARKET DAY, WATFORD, c. 1910

A weekly Tuesday market began here in the twelfth century. On the left-hand side are: Benskin's Watford Ales, a local branch whose eighteenth-century brewery was nearby; J, Mortimer's shop; the Spread Eagle public house; a row of stalls selling a wide range of goods and cattle tethered to the railings. On the opposite side of the street is Cawdell's shop. Today, Charters shopping centre dominates this part of High Street; the building with the cross on its roof is Etam and the one in the centre distance is the National Westminster Bank. The writer of this card, sent in 1916, was waiting for two Scottish soldiers who were to be billeted at her Bedford home.

(Published by Valentine & Sons, Dundee)

THE PARADE, WATFORD, c. 1906

Unfortunately, there were conflicting opinions as to the exact location of this view. Local residents could remember the tiled walls and marble counters of Sainsbury's shop – but could not remember where it was – both ends of High Street were suggested as likely locations. The old address of 5A High Street would place Sainsbury's emporium at the junction of Clarendon Road, where Clements store and Hatchards are today. Their smart assistants who knew their trade and gave good service are now at a premium. What a shame that this splendid Gothic pile had to come down! Every detail is interesting – unlike its replacement.

THE FIRE STATION, WATFORD, c. 1910

The 1910 directory gives the address of the Fire Station as 12A High Street. It was built after 1870, when this part of High Street was much improved. The lady cyclist – in full sail – would be passing modern development today, for nothing of this view remains. The Fire Station went in the 1950s, when Watford produced the first Town Plan. Amongst the landmarks swept away were a medicinal spring, a mechanic's reading room, some of the town's three schools and nine churches and chapels plus all the little alleyways leading off the High Street.

(Published by Blum & Degan, Kromo Series, London)

PHOTO. BY DOWNER & SONS, WATFORD.   COPYRIGHT.

THE GREAT LIBERAL MEETING AT THE CLARENDON HALL, WATFORD, JAN. 15TH. 1906.

LIBERAL MEETING AT CLARENDON HALL, WATFORD, 15th January 1906

Sir Henry Campbell-Bannerman led the Liberal landslide at the General Election of 1906. Mr. N. Micklem, K.C., the local candidate for West Hertfordshire, sat in the audience for this flashlight photograph. His long speech included some points with a contemporary ring:- "Nobody knew which way the Prime Minister had turned . . . . Why, with a strong cabinet and majority has he sent his Colonial Minister away? . . . . A poor man is not always dishonest . . . . find employment for men capable of work, funding it nationally, not locally. I don't care whether you call it Socialism." The reference is to Sir Arthur Balfour, Conservative Prime Minister from 1902–05.

(Published by Downer, Watford)

72020   **THE CANAL LOCK, WATFORD**   VALENTINES SERIES

THE CANAL LOCK, WATFORD, c. 1915

This photograph shows the Grand Junction Canal, which became the Grand Union Canal in 1929, when it was joined with seven other canals to form the Grand Union Canal system. Two narrow-boats are changing levels, with the horse grateful for a chance to feed whilst the boats, belonging to Fellows, Morton & Clayton Ltd., are negotiated through the lock. The woman wears a heavy shawl and head-cover although it seems to be one of the warmer months. Following the line of the rope, it is seen to be tied to the posts set in the boats' centre planks – obviously to keep the line of pull roughly parallel to the bank.

(Published by Valentine & Sons, Dundee)

FUNERAL OF MISS MARY MONEY AT WATFORD CEMETERY, OCTOBER 3RD, 1905.   *Downer, Photo.*

FUNERAL OF MISS MONEY, WATFORD CEMETERY, 3rd October, 1905

Accident, suicide or murder? Miss Mary Money, a 21-year-old spinster, who worked in Clapham, went out on Sunday evening, 24th September, 1905. Her mutilated body was found later, in Merstham tunnel. The inquest considered suicide or whether she had fallen or was thrown from the train. Watfordians, touched by the uncertain result, crowded the route of her funeral. Reverend Horne said: ". . . . we are troubled with a sense of something unintelligible, tragic, and mysterious which we cannot eliminate from our thoughts, explain or reconcile with what we think it should be".

(Published by Downer, Watford)

THE FAIR AT WOODSIDE, BRICKET WOOD, c. 1905

The Fair comes to Bricket Wood drawing vast crowds, including the St. Albans Boys' Brigade; shown with their white sashes. The people were able to try the swingboats, a steam roundabout, a magnificent helter-skelter and other amusements. All you needed for the helter-skelter was a halfpenny, a coconut mat – and courage! Here, one young lady is already halfway down. In Hertfordshire, the first July fair was Gooseberry Pudding Sunday, followed by five others before the 10th of the month – making July a busy time for the showman.

(Published by Downer, Watford)

The Station, Bricket Wood.

THE STATION, BRICKET WOOD, c. 1925

In the 1870 gazetteer, the full entry for the village reads: "Bricket Wood . . . . a railway station in Herts.; on the Watford and St. Albans railway". It seems unlikely that there were no houses or people although there is no mention of it in any other guide book. Here, the little station is seen from the road bridge and is looking south towards the cutting. There are some well-kept allotments between the platform and the road on the left. It is still part of the rail system between Watford and Garston.

RADLETT VILLIAGE

RADLETT, c. 1907

Although not issued until the 1920s, this is an earlier photograph from about 1907, when the population was about 1,200. The village grew when there was a general spread of population outwards from London. The view shows an archetypal High Street in the calm of the pre-motor era when domestic life merged with the public one. The flint-knapped house, on the left, looks ancient but only dates from 1852. Today, the Steak House opposite demonstrates another aspect of change and "improvement" to public houses. Beyond, the normal High Street facade of flat-fronted shops – belonging to the multiples – has taken over.

WATLING STREET, RADLETT, c. 1935

This classic view from the mid-1930s shows those "manor house" commercial buildings of the period between the wars. Barclays Bank still owns the building by the bus stop – another period touch. The flint-knapped shops beyond were built after the photograph on the previous page was taken – which is unusually late for this type of construction. The large awnings outside the shops have become smaller, ornamental ones. Even on a quiet Sunday morning, the traffic never ceases on this road – the A5 – once the Watling Street constructed by the Romans.

SCHOOLS AND CHURCH, RADLETT, c. 1908

Christ Church has been extended – probably twice – and now presents a revised shape from the original design of 1864. Today, the school, built in 1878, is screened from view by arboreal growth but, being flint, is just the same as in this picture. It now functions as a Youth and Community Centre and the gate and post-box have gone. The quiet road – now the busy A5 – separates the church from the churchyard which is across the road on the right and not visible here.

(Published by Coles, Watford)

OLD HOUSES AT LETCHMORE HEATH.

Downer & Sons, Photo.

OLD HOUSES, LETCHMORE HEATH, c. 1904

These battered dwellings, with hollyhocks at the door, holes in the gable and locals passing the time of day, were at an unknown location in the village and would need extensive research to establish the exact site. They have gone and, like many Edwardian cards, depict a bygone age that could be called picturesque, existing only in the memories of older residents – and on contemporary photographs and postcards. This card was sent by Flo, a domestic servant, to Rosie who was also in service and worked in Portland Place, London.

(Published by Downer, Watford)

LETCHMORE HEATH, HERTS.

LETCHMORE HEATH, c. 1920

Unfortunately, it has also been impossible to discover the location of this view on a typical sepia postcard of the 1920s, issued by a local newsagent, F. A. Hood, whose shop is shown on the right. This is a picture-book village, nowadays full of Sunday lunch-time visitors and their cars. It was thought that the scene must be opposite the entrance to Bhaktivedanta Manor – but it is not. A local resident suggested that this property was brought down by a string of bombs during World War 2 and this seems to be the most likely explanation.

(Published by The R.A.P. Co. Ltd., London and F. A. Hood, Letchmore Heath)

THE HEADMASTER'S HOUSE, ALDENHAM SCHOOL

THE SCHOOL AND HEADMASTER'S HOUSE, ALDENHAM, c. 1918

Founded in 1597 by Richard Platt, a London brewer, the school was built to educate children of poor people from Aldenham and children of the Freemen of the Company of Brewers, London. It was rebuilt and enlarged in the nineteenth century, producing this Jacobean-style building with castellated battlements, and completed by 1888. A new chapel, designed by W. G. Newton, was added just before World War 2 and it now houses two 1958 paintings by that eccentric genius from Cookham – Stanley Spencer.

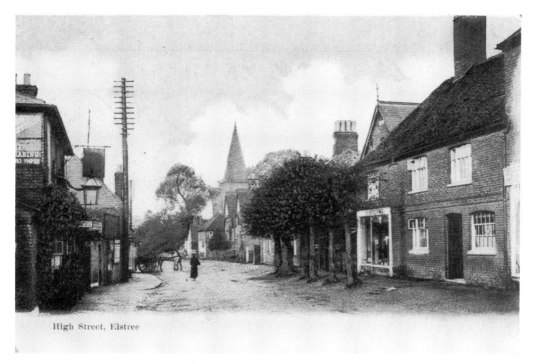

High Street, Elstree

HIGH STREET, ELSTREE, c. 1905

From the Plough public house – on the left – this view down the High Street is relatively unchanged, but no longer a haven of rural peace. A horse in the same position today would definitely be in a hazardous position! Behind the trees on the right-hand side is the Creamery which, together with other shops on that side, has a brand new front. The 1876 chapel, adjacent to the Creamery, has been whitewashed. Further down, the gabled house before the church is now Hertsmere Progressive Synagogue and faces some new flats on the left-hand side.

ELSTREE STATION, M. RLY.

ELSTREE STATION, c. 1908

The town's name, so boldly displayed here for travellers, was given in King Offa's grant and translates as "Eagles' Grove". Situated on the Midland Railway line, this station served a small population – only about 500 in 1908. Note the gas-mantled lamps, the train from London under its own steam, and the lack of advertising. The station was a mile from Elstree but it also served the growing population of Boreham Wood which was nearer. It is now known as Elstree and Boreham Wood station and has electric gantries bridging the tracks.

Shenley Road, Boreham Wood.

SHENLEY ROAD, BOREHAM WOOD, c. 1915

The postcard shows a scene that is barely recognisable today. Modern development has altered all the properties except the four shops at the junction of Drayton Road on the right. In this scene of Bass and bassinet, beer is being delivered by a horse-drawn dray – a policeman is keeping watch over the unattended barrels in the road. The public house may still be there – embedded in the new shop-fronts at the top of the road. The Sainsbury complex is further along on the left-hand side.

SHENLEY. The White Horse Hotel.

THE WHITE HORSE HOTEL, SHENLEY, c. 1910

This Edwardian hotel is the only one in the village that is original. It now has a mass of wisteria, window boxes and tubs of conifers on the front. Doors have been filled in and new ones added. The old shed has been pulled down to give access to the ear park. The large tree on the right marks the location of a Garden Centre.

KING WILLIAM THE FOURTH, SHENLEY. The prettiest spot in Herts. Alpha, St. Albans.
(Five miles from St. Albans. Five miles from Barnet.)

KING WILLIAM THE FOURTH, SHENLEY, c. 1905

What a wonderful card! A good view of the pub; an interesting sign; an unusual rig; many locals, including bonny babies in bonnets and "old boys" – even a table with a jug of flowers! George Watts, the licensee, was having a busy day. The pub was rebuilt in a black and white half-timbered style in c. 1958. It is still a busy pub today, under the Irish eye of Martin Guidera, the present landlord. The message on this postcard is a bonus: "Dear S, Don't forget a small bit of lime for me. Put it in a small cocoa tin, if you have one, W.J.R.", August 1906.

(Published by Alpha, St. Albans)

THE OLD CAGE, SHENLEY, c. 1905

Situated on the village green, the title refers to the old beehive-shaped lock-up, built to restrain the "roaring boys" and other ne'er-do-wells. It has two small plaques bearing the homilies "DO WELL AND FEAR NOT" and "BE SOBER BE VIGILANT"; the pointed door has been replaced and the exterior has been cement rendered. It is still uninviting! On the left is the old Queen public house, demolished in 1924 and replaced by a new one called the Queen Adelaide. The white cottage between the pub and the lock-up was pulled down to make way for the car park entrance.

P.15490 NAPSBURY HOSPITAL, NEAR ST. ALBANS, HERTS.

NAPSBURY HOSPITAL, NEAR ST. ALBANS, c. 1952

Just outside London Colney, off the Shenley Road, Napsbury Hospital was built in 1905 by Rowland Plumbe. Its distinctive shape is most apparent when viewed from the air; on the ground, such a large complex defies investigation.

(Published by Aero Pictorial Ltd., London)

2, Peahen Buildings, London Road, St. Albans.

2, PEAHEN BUILDINGS, LONDON ROAD, ST. ALBANS, c. 1906

This advertising postcard must have been issued by the shopkeeper for the printed message, on the reverse, proudly extols the services provided for The Prince of Wales and the general public. The shop-front is beautifully appointed. In the window, there is a most elaborate dress and a sign advertising their blind-cleaning service. The advertisement on the back of the card states ". . . .Boas, Feathers, Gloves . . . beautifully Cleaned. . . . High-Class Work, Moderate Prices". Now renumbered, the shop must be at 20, London Road, a newsagents, the only shop to have a raked doorway and to match the pattern of this upper storey.

(Published by G. Wright & Sons, St. Albans)

ST ALBANS   HOLYWELL HILL.

Photochrom Co., Ltd., London.

HOLYWELL HILL, ST. AßLBANS, c. 1903

This view is looking up the hill towards the city centre; the River Ver is seen on the left, just before it flows beneath the road bridge. In the centre is the White Hart, a fifteenth-century building which has been altered constantly and conceals its early origins. The Jacobite, Lord Lovat, on his way to the Tower, was drawn by the artist William Hogarth, at this inn. Sarah, Duchess of Marlborough was born at Holywell. The Holy Well is nearby, in the playing fields of St. Albans School. Good Georgian houses still line this entrance to the city but traffic problems have necessitated the addition of a roundabout at this junction.

(Published by Photochrom Co. Ltd., London)

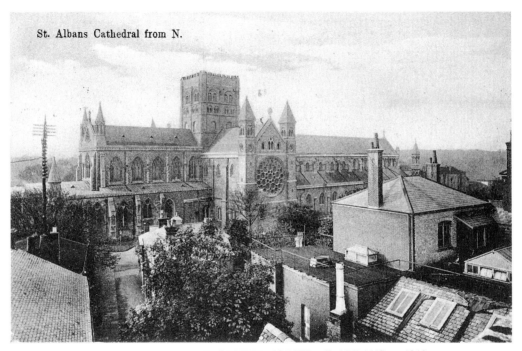

St. Albans Cathedral from N.

THE CATHEDRAL FROM THE NORTH, ST. ALBANS, c. 1910

Much of the eleventh-century abbey can be seen on this view. The North Transept – the reputed site of St. Alban's martyrdom – and wall beyond are Abbot Paul's work, using bricks from Verulamium. The fabric of the Abbey proceeded in three stages: main body 1077–89; western extensions 1195–1235 and eastern extensions 1256–1400. Little changed until Lord Grimthorpe's repairs and restorations in 1856–77 which added pointed tops to the previously battlemented towers. He is reputed to have spent almost £140,000 of his own money – not only for these repairs but also on the gift of the large stone pulpit in the nave.

KING OFFA'S FRESCO, ST. ALBANS ABBEY, c. 1959

Offa, King of Mercia, obtained leave of the Pope to build an abbey on the site of a small church. The abbey stood from the eighth century until 1077, when it was rebuilt by Paul of Caen. This fifteenth-century painting is over the arch leading to the North Transept from the Presbytery aisle; the 1950s photograph, used for this postcard, is of such quality that the details on the fresco are clearly seen. This is a symbolic portrait rather than a likeness; nevertheless, it resembles the Offa portait in "The Life of St. Alban" in Trinity College, Dublin. There, Offa is shown with two advisors watching two workmen hod-carrying and another man pushing a wheelbarrow.

(Published by Walter Scott, Bradford)

101

YE OLD ROUND HOUSE, ST. ALBANS, c. 1910

The search for an unusual card of a famous tourist spot is always a challenge. This real photographic postcard of the Old Fighting Cocks is such a card. The inclusion of the landlord and barmaids adds a personal touch to the usual "tourist view". Any building that Pevsner describes as remarkable must have merit. This octagonal, timber-framed building was once a monastic fish lodge, built on a gatehouse, and has also served as a dovecote and a cock-pit. It has been an inn since the Dissolution and is one of England's oldest inns. Its peaceful position, close to the abbey grounds, may have helped to preserve its sixteenth-century origins.

Old Silk Mill, St. Albans.

THE OLD SILK MILL, ST. ALBANS, c. 1906

The rear view of the distinctive Old Fighting Cocks, in the background, identifies this area of St. Albans as the bottom of Abbey Mill Lane, with the old Silk Mill – mentioned in the caption – just out of sight, on the right-hand side. The bridge has been replaced by a brick one, constructed in 1931. The rural aspect now resembles a small park.

(Published by Chester Vaughan, London)

THE SILK MILL, ST. ALBANS. (35)

THE SILK MILL, ST. ALBANS, c. 1910

This time the publisher has managed to feature the Silk Mill in the picture! Built on the site of the old abbey mill, this was an eighteenth-century building that manufactured silk. It had nine bays and was three storeys high. "Catch before it goes" was never more true a saying – for the mill is in the process of being converted and the building with the mansard roof together with the squarish warehouse, have already been demolished. The days of straw-plaiting and silk weaving in the city are numbered!

THE ROMAN THEATRE, VERULAMIUM, ST. ALBANS, c. 1950

Hollywood's vast Roman circuses are at odds with the reality of Roman Verulamium's small theatre. Excavated by Miss K. Kenyon, C.B.E., D.Lit., F.B.A., in 1934, it was found that, in A.D. 180, alterations put seats across the stage front that had three sets of steps down to a rectangular area. The stage was fronted by five columns and had four entrances at its rear. The whole arena had circular seating. Being near the Temple, it was used for religious ceremonies and every other kind of entertainment – indeed, the central post suggests that animals were tied there prior to baiting. Philosophers and poets alike, loved to saunter among the ruined fragments. Sir Thomas More wanted to live and die here.

VERULAMIUM – THE ROMAN THEATRE

THE CLOCK TOWER, ST. ALBANS,
c. 1910

One of the rare survivals of an English belfry, the fifteenth-century Clock Tower stands at the city's centre. French Row is on its left and Market Place on the right. Mediæval and Victorian styles rub shoulders. On the left is the restored Fleur-de-Lis Inn which, tradition has it, was named for King John of France who was imprisoned here after the Battle of Poitiers in 1356. The large Victorian Corn Exchange is on the right of this birds-eye view of the area. A closer view of the market has been used for the front cover illustration. The postcard was sent to a Miss Tait to advise her that her birthday box had been sent with the carriers, Carter Paterson.

(Published by Valentine & Sons, Dundee)

FRENCH ROW, ST. ALBANS. c. 1935

A closer view of this narrow mediæval street shows the details of pre-reformation construction. The crooked over-hanging upper storey, on the right, is next to the Fleur-de-Lis inn and can be seen on the previous picture. Nos. 1–5 once made up the Christopher Inn, the oldest best-known and most notorious hostelry of all 32 pubs in the city. Towns usually grow up around the main church and then spread out; in St. Albans, the geography meant that streets meandered along the contours, so nothing is straight and seven roads converge here – making it easy for tourists to explore. This row now accommodates up-market shops that have been tastefully incorporated into the street scene.

(Published by Valentine & Sons, Dundee)

Market Cross, St. Albans

60061

MARKET CROSS, ST. ALBANS, c. 1909

Another view looking towards the Clock Tower – but from the other side – also shows a section of High Street with the Abbey behind. The name Market Cross is a reference to one of those erected to mark Queen Eleanor's funeral progress towards Waltham – it was pulled down in 1703. This 1909 view shows a very unusual timber-hauling rig; the seventeenth-century Boot, on the left, was selling Sedgwicks Ales, brewed in Watford and was just an ale house. Opposite was H. Lee's salt merchant's shop – a mediæval trade. This shop has endured and is now a corn chandler's premises.

(Published by Valentine & Sons, Dundee)

TOWN HALL AND ST. PETER'S STREET, ST. ALBANS, c. 1904

At the end of Market Place, facing St. Peter's Street, is George Smith's Town Hall of 1830 – which is so like Bishop Stortford's Corn Exchange of 1828. The grand Ionic columns and Tuscan pillars – supported on a plinth in the best Greek style – signify the growth of St. Albans from country town to urban community. The street that leads into the distance on the left is Chequer Street. On the right are the small shops of St. Peter's Street with the White Horse on the extreme right. This silver bromide postcard was produced because the Post Office refused to carry similar ones made of aluminium. It is from a set of six views of the city.

(Published by Raphael Tuck & Sons, Silverette Series, London)

ST. PETER'S STREET, ST. ALBANS, c. 1904

In Roman times, this area was the venue for their chariot races. In more recent years, Hiring Fairs were held in this wide street. Every October, labourer's, seeking a year's work, wore tokens of their trade in their hats. When agreement was reached, a shilling was given as a contract for a wage of 15/- (75p) per week and a tied cottage; boys as young as nine or ten years of age were hired under the same system. Nowadays, residents are satisfied with the Saturday market! This is a view of the street from the Town Hall and the White Horse is on the extreme left. This western flank of the street retained these facades until the 1950s and 1960s, when shop fronts were altered and chain-stores moved into the street. The middle rank of trees has also gone.

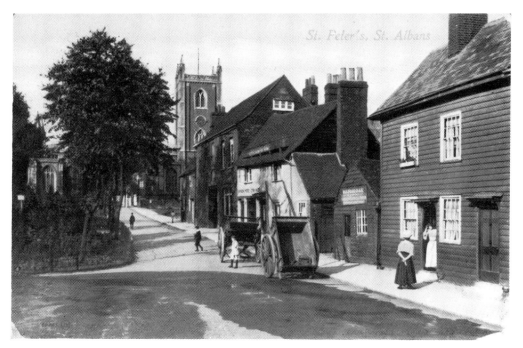

ST. PETER'S CHURCH, ST. ALBANS, c. 1910

Church Gardens leads to St. Peter's Church, another building that was restored in the Victorian style by Lord Grimsthorpe. The boarded cottages used to stand at the junction of Hatfield Road – where the Blacksmith Arms is now. The next two buildings have also gone and the premises beyond are now occupied by Rumball Sedgwick. Unfortunately, the printing process used for these coloured cards does not give a very sharp image so the words on the sign on the small shed are indistinct. It appears to read – "H.C. Page R & S" – but the rest is illegible. The two carts were probably owned by the firm. On the right, two ladies are enjoying a chat in the early evening sunlight.

(Published by Valentine & Sons, Dundee)

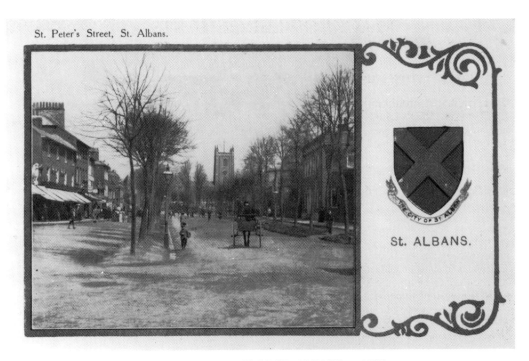

St. Peter's Street, St. Albans.

St. ALBANS.

THE COAT OF ARMS OF ST. ALBANS, c. 1905

In heraldry, the simple form denotes the most ancient usage. The city's coat of arms has a very basic design – an azure escutcheon charged with a gold saltire. It is symbolic of charity, wealth and generosity. To complete the design on this heraldic postcard, there is a view of St. Peter's Street which emphasises its width.

(Published by Stoddart & Co., Ja-Ja Series, Grimsby)

We hope you have enjoyed this first "tour" of Hertfordshire and look forward to visiting the central, eastern and northern parts of the county in Volumes II and III.

ACKNOWLEDGEMENTS

The authors wish to recognise the assistance given by the following people:-

The Librarian, Watford Library;
The Librarian, King's Langley Library;
Our daughter, Helen;
All those local residents who helped with directions, information and anecdotes.

Gillian Jackson, for editing the text.

Steve Benz, for additional editing and marketing.

THE AUTHORS

Margaret Sturgess was born in Harpenden, Herts. She is a counsellor at the Citizens Advice Bureau. Her interests are embroidery, gardening and the social history of domestic servants. Roy Sturgess was born in Southend-on-Sea, Essex. He is a retired Life Assurance Supervisor. His interests are music, art, writing, ephemera, philately, gardening and the painting and designing of postcards. He is publicity officer of Peterborough & District Postcard Club. Margaret and Roy were married in 1956 and have lived in Peterborough for twenty years. They have one daughter – Helen – who is a Principal Speech Therapist.

BIBLIOGRAPHY

Pictorial Guide to Hertfordshire, Eric G. Meadows. White Crescent Press.

The King's England – Hertfordshire, Arthur Mee. Hodder & Stoughton.

The Buildings of England – Hertfordshire, Nicholas Pevsner.
            2nd Edition revised by Bridget Cherry. Penguin Books (1977)

Herts. & Bucks., S. E. Winbolt. Penguin Books (1949)

Victorian & Edwardian Hertfordshire from old photographs, Richard Whitmore. Batsford (1976)

Hertfordshire Headlines, Richard Whitmore. Countryside Books (1987)

The Folklore of Hertfordshire, Doris Jones-Baker. Batsford (1977)

Hertfordshire Photographers 1839–1939, compiled by Bill Smith & Michael Pritchard. 2nd Edit. (1985)

History of England, edited by Sir Ifor Evans. Methuen (1957)

The Imperial Gazetteer of England and Wales. 6 vols., John Marius Wilson. A. Fullerton & Co. (1870)

Concise Dictionary of National Biography. O.U.P. (1930)

A Book of Days. 2 vols. Chambers (1869)

Picture Postcards and their Publishers, Anthony Byatt. A. Byatt (1978)